D1245587

Praise for Jesus Walks the Southland...

In *Jesus Walks the Southland*, Robert Gray paints a triptych of the holy Trinity of the South—religion, racism, and politics. And, as "The Power of Prayer" signals, the painting is a personal prayer of a white Southerner offered as liturgy for others to recite. If before you devour the collection you want to know whether the prayer is lament, confession or thanksgiving, the answer is a powerful yes.

> Rev. O. Wesley Allen, Jr., author of *The Renewed Homiletic* and *Reading the Synoptic Gospels*

Rob Gray's poems rethink that holy relation of poet to place, as he offers what he calls fragments, a set of psalms to displace the old songs of the Southland. Rob is a product of his time, writing for his time, the Saint Paul of Alabama sitting at his keyboard "trying / trying" to decode the dialectic of despair and guilt, the tangle of race and complicity, the "whiteness / silently blinding us to the life of things." He mingles metaphysics, mourning, reverse code-switching, and a haunted respect for what he understands but cannot know. A necessary collection of poems.

> Trish Harris, editor of *The Pea River Journal*

Jesus Walks the Southland takes the reader on an emotional journey. In this collection, Robert Gray shows the reader just what it is like to be a white male struggling to make sense of the south he loves, in spite of some of its contradictory behavior as it relates to race, religion and politics. The poems in this collection are a mixture of irony, self-reflection and hope that will leave the reader pining for more glimpses into the mind of this talented, insightful poet.

> Angela Jackson-Brown, author of *Drinking From A Bitter Cup*

In Rob Gray's *Jesus Walks the Southland*, we become the listener to a skeptical, candid conversation about the twin pillars of Southern complexity: race and religion. Gray pulls no punches in cataloging the perverse things done in Jesus' name and the political manipulations that "find / ways to bring / people / together / to hate / in the name of love." Perhaps Gray's most ambitious effort is to save Christ from Christianity. Ultimately, these poems rely on a redemptive quality of poetry and of a religious life rooted in the secular world. I admire the courage, honesty, and clarity of vision of these poems.

> Hank Lazer, author of *The New Spirit*

Jesus Walks the Southland is a phenomenal testimony to the trials of the human spirit, when the reality of the beauty and blatant hypocrisy of its spiritual, social and political environment are tested. Whether describing the beautiful geographical landscapes of Alabama or exploring the dark and ugly exploitations of a racist Jim Crow past, Gray takes the reader on a spiritual and geographical journey that possesses the realism of a Norman Rockwell painting but with a Thoreau-like flow. Regardless of your race, sex, spiritual beliefs, or geographical location, you'll love this book. It speaks to the human in us all.

> Alex "Huggy Bear" Lofton, spoken word artist and author of "Bama"

There is a four-way intersection where spirituality, sincerity, empathy and beauty meet and that is where you will find Rob Gray's poetry. These poems are for those who love God, nature and justice and are not afraid to come right out and say it.

Barry Marks, author of *Sounding* and *Possible Crocodiles*

You won't find any other book of poetry like this. Brilliant and brief lines of free verse—alliterative, allusive, and arresting, with an up-to-the-minute politics of social justice. This is Ginsberg without the Howl, making a protest that serves justice better in these times. Teachers now teach about privilege and internalized oppression and the politics of location, but where are the poets to hold people, to mirror them to themselves, during these difficult learnings? Gray is such a poet; he makes common cause with readers in these direct, declarative poems that let us follow him into difficult places and see some of the outrage and the hypocrisies that fuel his passion for justice. His silent ally is Christ who walks these pages wounded by what is done in his name, yet still present, waiting to be known, and sometimes divined intuitively. Gray mines English literature dazzlingly, alluding to many authors and ideas, while he journeys right up and into the fraught racial crises of Here-and-Now, in us and around us, which he has the bravery to name and stay with, in brief words and simple lines. I think that like "Howl," this book will make literary history.

Peggy McIntosh, author of "White Privilege: Unpacking the Invisible Knapsack"

This is a book about feeling, and Gray touches difficult subjects with a soft hand to balance a heavy heart with a steady voice. These poems tour the hypocrisy of a landscape wild with blood and bibles—how love, even in the Christian sense, in the south has so little to do with God. Rather than take us head on, Gray takes us to the side and asks us to listen. It is a welcome move. Perhaps what is the greatest triumph here is that these poems refuse to postulate—what the speaker sees and hears is what you get—and from that we can feel our way through a southern experience that questions what in any of us could possibly be holy. And if the questions are difficult it is only because the answers are worse, that we pretend that we live without feeling a thing.

Ray McManus, author of *Punch* and *Red Dirt Jesus*

Robert Gray's new book walks through the kudzu-draped landscape of the southern struggle with race and religion "in muffled rustles and hushed whispers." Gray reminds us that Jesus "came to write new worlds / with imagination and love" but that even poets must wrestle with making sense of a culture unable to see the similarity between coal and diamond or to fully account for the blood in the trees. For Gray, "poems happen in the dark." These poems, however, are limned with light; they are richly allusive and politically engaged, challenging our assumptions about southern structures of thought and asking us to do battle with the "whiteness / silently blinding us to the life of things."

Patti White, author of *Chain Link Fence*

Jesus Walks the Southland

JESUS WALKS THE SOUTH LAND

ROBERT GRAY

Negative Capability
PRESS
MOBILE, ALABAMA

Jesus Walks the Southland

Copyright © 2014, Robert Gray

Cover and Interior Design by Megan Cary
Author photo by Robert Brown

ISBN 978-0-942544-94-7
Library of Congress Control Number: 2014936719

Negative Capability Press
62 Ridgelawn Drive East
Mobile, Alabama 36608
(251) 591-2922

www.negativecapabilitypress.org
facebook.com/negativecapabilitypress

For my children, Liam and Emma

And for Bonnie

May they persist in the struggle against the darkness that casts itself as light…

TABLE OF CONTENTS

ONE: IT'S DIFFERENT GROWING UP IN THE SOUTH   1

The Day I Was Born   3

Lost Cause   4

I Wish That I Were Langston Hughes   5

The Road to the Lake   8

Humidity   10

To Sing of the South   11

Good Little Girl   12

Architectural Inequities   14

The Good of Poems   15

Love Poem #1   16

Love Poem #2   17

Scars of Segregation   18

A Hymn to Post-Racial America   19

All the Sacredness of Life   20

Persistence of the Dialectic   21

Our Country Is Broken   22

A Hymn to American Difference   24

TWO: JESUS WALKS THE SOUTHLAND   25

Jesus Walks the Southland   27

From Cross to Empty Tomb   28

Building Kingdoms   29

Steeples   31

My Brand New Bible   32

The Power of Prayer   34

A Poem for William Blake   35

These Things Aren't Easy   36

The Road to Demopolis 37

The Holiness Temple of Immaculate Redemption 40

Funeral in Early Spring 41

Sermon on the Mount circa 2008 43

Rapture 45

The War on Christianity 46

Part of God's Inconceivable Plan 47

When We Made God 48

A Word in the Beginning 49

THREE: AND THE WORD WAS GOD 51

Twilight 53

Poems Happen in the Dark 54

The Life of Things 55

Smoky Mountain Stream 56

Cathedral 58

When I Sing 59

Beyond the Margins 61

Azalea Spring 63

On Letting Go the Transcendental Signified 64

Sunset on Mobile Bay 65

Just Off the End of the Pier 66

Of Schools and Schoolmasters 67

Jim's Place 68

Obsequies of Autumn 69

Rhyming Landscapes 70

Deep Thoughts 71

When Skies Are Grey 73

NOTES 75

ONE

It's Different Growing
Up in the South

The Day I Was Born

whenever i say i'm from alabama
people seem to want to ask
what it was like to hold that fire hose
if i ever had to answer i'd tell them
i was born the day that happened

they seem to want to ask
what it was like to bomb that church
and kill those little girls
i was born that day as well

i was born the day they marched across
the edmund pettus bridge
the day wallace made his stand
the day martin had his dream
the day he saw the mountaintop
and the day after that

i was born innocent
free of all the blood
shed that day
but i was born into blood
i still am washing from my hands

LOST CAUSE

in a few thousand years
when the remnant
fragments of our lost
civilization sift
through the fingers
of an eager archaeologist

will she feel after all
the documents and dvds
the rage that runs through
the credit cards and christmas
lights the empty tea bags
coffee cups and jesus prints

and later when she moves
a mile or so downhill
and finds blood stains
bullet holes and shards of glass
from shattered photos
of lost loved ones scattered
across a book left open
to a page with words in red

will she sense this rage
as a seething symptom
of the dark contrasts of
a divided culture a symptom
cultivated to stand as cause
so it might seep out
in segregated spaces
and take the blame

I WISH THAT I WERE
LANGSTON HUGHES

or even maya angelou
able to cry out for freedom
over the roofs of the world
from a position of surprising
and unaccustomed strength
but sadly i am not
for no matter how much
i read or think or discuss
no matter how enlightened i may feel
i can never understand
as a white poet
privileged if by nothing else
but my own whiteness
how the truth in their words
can see so well into the life of things
and so i am damned
by that same whiteness
always to be disadvantaged
always impoverished

i have long found
a fundamental difference
between white poetry
and black poetry
and i have often envied it
and while i am certainly
as guilty as anyone and
would never wish to oversimplify
it seems to me that white poetry
has often soared on the ethereal
wings of imagination and philosophy

with a mission to explore
the deep and hidden meanings
of the heights of heaven
in order that poets might
as prophets or amanuenses
bring the mountaintop down
so that truth might come to be
within the reach of those
of us too blind or deaf
to write the zeitgeist of eternity
and so white poets have pontificated
throughout history on the wherefores
and whys of our existence
almost as if poets and poetry
had nothing else or better to do

african american poetry
on the other hand
has preferred to labor
with its hands in the earth
it has done its work
in the everyday
at the dinner table
or through childhood remembrances
born out of minds too strewn
with petty cares
or while standing on
the grave of dreams
deferred from the earth's inside
this voice of the subaltern
long subjected to the margins
has preferred to work
down in the midst of things
where life happens
lifting truth up to the heavens

in an act of heavy praise
for there is power in pain
and strangled possibility
but there is also beauty
in the fact of blackness
just as there is poetry
in the song of a caged bird
or the lies of a mask
perhaps even more than
in the tortured thoughts
of an overly pensive prince
or an overwrought
ideological wasteland

this privilege of pondering
life's mysteries by deconstructing
the semantics of our social
discourses in a vain hope that
by revealing and reversing
historical and hierarchical binaries
they might dry up or explode
is a privilege wrought
with hidden costs and effects
that we are taught not to see
many might argue that poetry
should be above the baseness
of politics and there may well be
a richness to those arguments
but there is also a whiteness
silently blinding us to the life of things

THE ROAD TO THE LAKE

before the four-lane was finished
the road to the lake
rose and fell and wound through
trees so draped with kudzu
they looked like elephants
lined up to drink
from the shimmery mirages
that danced fleetingly
on the sun-grey pavement

we would usually stop
just out of town
at the shelton creek bait company
to pick up crickets candy and worms
that is
if we hadn't already hit
yonder's blossom
before leaving town

we'd then bypass the weogufka vf&w
hustle past hanover rockford and hissop
before turning off onto a series
of county routes
country roads of the first order
a watercolorist's paradise
unruly fields framed by
walls of gossiping woods
speaking the stories of the south
in muffled rustles and hushed whispers
fields punctuated
by a majestic weathered oak
a solitary shack's rusted roof

propped on rotting paintless planks
that concealed appalling
poverty white and black
just behind rustic walls

we would ride right past
distracted by desires
seductively luring us
to blue waters
distracted by discourses
silently teaching us
to behold these landscapes
as scenes of charm and beauty
they and we
captured in watercolor

HUMIDITY

growing up in the south

i was well into my teens before
i realized what humidity is

don't get me wrong i knew

the textbook definition i
understood what they were talking

about when they talked about it

on the news but to me that was just
what air felt like air was supposed

to confront you when you walk

outside it was supposed to engulf
you in smothering draining stifling

warmth like a womb but without

nurture or comfort it was something
invisible unnoticed hanging over you heavy

like a sheet damp from an anxious

restless night so native to the environment
so pervasive in our structures so natural

it was almost like racism

To Sing of the South

for michael donald

i sing of a south
of loblolly pine
where faithful facades
transform into gods
where blood hangs
from trees like memory

i sing of a south
of live oak and moss
where attitudes change
but privilege remains
where blood hangs
from trees like memory

i sing of a south
of magnolia and ash
where too empty lives
fill too many graves
where blood hangs
from trees like memory

i sing of a south
of dogwood and camphor
where jesus and justice
are preached more than practiced
and memory stains
trees with blood

GOOD LITTLE GIRL

she reads her bible every day
a red gideon's that sits beside her alarm
each morning scans a verse or two

thinks how much she likes
the way its cover reminds her
of the blood of jesus

and how it matches
almost perfectly the roses
on her laura ashley comforter

she makes a point to be a good christian
believes god's favor will help her get ahead
achieve lofty ambitions and expectations

she wants the life her parents have
exclusive neighborhood and country club
a vacation home at the beach

she writes her congressman often
urging him to keep god first
and take our country back

from those who have taken it away
the godless liberals and gays
and those too lazy to get a job

she tells him to get government out of our lives
because we can't afford to keep giving
everything this country has to the poor

she asks him to cut her daddy's taxes
and push harder for school vouchers
because it costs so much for private school

where she can have a safe enriching environment
that will give her a better chance in the world
plus she needs a school where god's allowed inside

she prays to jesus every night
asking him to take away her troubles
and heal this broken world

she asks him for a bimmer birthday present
more popularity at school
and a better ivy league scholarship offer

because she's a good girl who reads her bible every day

Architectural Inequities

it's been forty years since i started
first grade at main avenue school
built forty years earlier

about the time my dad was born
about the time *to kill a mockingbird* was set
it seemed so much older than it should have

so much older than it should seem now
a vacant lot for almost thirty years
but my only remaining memories

of that old building are the water fountains
and how i never understood
why they always seemed to come in twos

one a tall metallic box with water
nicely chilled the other's water warmed
by ambient heat beneath the floor

shiny ceramic white like the urinals
in the boys' room reeking with the putrid stench
from forty years of careless aim

THE GOOD OF POEMS

what good are poems
to corporal erin scott
lying dead in the sand
at twenty-three
the random victim
of a rocket-propelled
grenade attack
on her third tour in iraq
an arbitrary sacrifice
to ideological hatred
and callous ignorance

what good are poems
to young avondre adams
shot on the sidewalk
as he played across the street
from his big momma's house
trapped in a crossfire
of systemic oppression
and deep-rooted hopelessness

what good is poetry
in a world where nothing
can slow the violence
senseless brutality
and indifferent blindness that
prevents us all from sharing in it

Love Poem #1

i am ready
for a politics of love
but i don't believe
the christians would
go for it
a politics where
politicians no longer use
hate to unite
their constituencies

once they used race
but now they've turned
to jesus
to values
to tradition
ways to find
ways to bring
people
together
to hate
in the name of love

Love Poem #2

just as racism
is no longer
about color
but privilege
pervading
color's absence
christianity
would seem
no longer
about love

SCARS OF SEGREGATION

scars still starkly mark
the map of old mobile
ancient racial scars
scars of segregation
seen in the streets
in anonymous eyes
looks of anger regret
and resentment
linger from the residue
of separation and
inequality remaining
indelibly marked
in countless eager minds
extinguished dreams
and put out possibilities

schools created in the name
of christ cripple public schools
disabling opportunity for many
whose color or class consign
them to lives confined
by unwritten lines on every map

if education really is
the lighting of a fire
why must the fuel
ever be a cross

A Hymn to Post-Racial America

as a young man walked
through an exclusive neighborhood

in the exclusive suburbs west of town

a middle-aged man
out to check his mail asked

the young man what he was doing

in this part of town
the young man politely replied

it's a free country so the older man

as if to prove it's not
went inside to call the cops

ALL THE SACREDNESS OF LIFE

as a middle-aged couple walks
through downtown a young man

approaches pulls a gun and takes their cash

as the young man turns and runs the older man
calls *you're making a big mistake son*

the young man turns around walks slowly back and shouts

i ain't your motherfuckin' son points the gun
in the other's face and pulls the trigger

dead

this young man stands an icon for his race
for tragic disregard for human life

while we collective icons of our own

want answers but won't apprehend
the disregarded sacredness of his

PERSISTENCE OF THE DIALECTIC

in a world where diamonds and coal
are genetically the same

where diamonds are sculpted
to shine set as ornamentation

valued privileged revered
where coal must do the work must

be consumed by the processes
of powering our world

and cast out as detritus as pollution
let there be justice at last

OUR COUNTRY IS BROKEN

our country is broken and
never has it been more evident
than now that democracy
is collective mediocrity
when every day brings
a brand new crop of idiotic emails
and facebook posts
forwarding insipid distasteful
doses of ignorance hatred and evil
under the ruse of rightness and religion

this mindless appalling
attack on truth serves
narrow elite interests
carefully crafted to appeal
to the common masses
through the sinister prostitution
of righteous indignation
under the guise of godliness
rendering the dispossessed
middle classes as nothing
more than industrious sheep

it mocks the historic lines
underlying lady liberty
undergirding what is supposed
to constitute our national greatness
while those who cry out for the
poor the tired the tempest-tossed
those who cry out against the madness
are cast aside as madmen crying out
in the marketplace which

in our modern metaphysic
has become the seeming
sepulcher of god

our country is broken
our country remains broken
and we have broken it

A HYMN TO AMERICAN DIFFERENCE

there used to be a myth
of the melting pot where
all americans of various

nationalities would come
together as one
but the new concoction

began to darken some
groups couldn't melt at all
so we had to find a new metaphor

first we tried a tapestry
and then we found a quilt
it seemed more democratic

more genuinely american
it didn't catch on
so we had to settle on a salad bowl

a multicultural combination
of flavors bound together
with a nice ranch dressing

but then we pushed it further
it's now better to be color blind
an interesting return to the melting pot

a brilliant cynical attempt
at a mystical alchemy binding all
together in an alloy of ideology

a blinding hope that all colors
combined together
will still shine white

TWO

Jesus Walks the Southland

Jesus Walks the Southland

tonight i saw jesus
in my rearview mirror
he was on the side
of the road in montgomery
and looked just like
he always did
in those paintings
except that he was
a bit thinner on top
and a lot dirtier
which i guess was
just from the shit
that's been dumped
on him recently
i couldn't really tell
if he was hitchhiking
or just walking along
it all happened too fast
but it wouldn't have mattered
anyway because i wasn't looking
out for him besides
i had somewhere to get to
and didn't have room in my car

FROM CROSS TO EMPTY TOMB

two potential symbols
for a movement destined
to change the world

the first stood
as an instrument
of roman brutality
domination and death
an object lesson for
those who challenged
imperial dominion

the second
with much softer
insinuations signified
maternal love
womb-like deliverance
rebirth redemption
resurrection

how different might
the movement be
how different the world
had patriarchs given
themselves to wisdom
and left the thunderbolt
of zeus alone

BUILDING KINGDOMS

for jim flowers

once we forgot
that all gods
all deities reside
inside the human breast

we created a god
in our image
and confined him
to imaginary realms

further forgetting
the proper place
and function of god
is human communion

so jesus came
to tear down empires
and institutions
built on our forgetfulness

came to write new worlds
with imagination and love
but new institutions
bearing his name

and an imperialism
of empiricism erected
in error new empires for
their imaginary god

but all jesus wanted
was simply to remind us
that the only way to
the kingdom he spoke of

is through purposeful
acts of imagination
the mind doing
the work of the heart

STEEPLES

as i sit here
in a catholic church
parking lot
feeling
power
protruding
from a pronounced
architectural
celebration
of the maleness
of god
i discern
discourses
of dominion
disseminating
to the masses
a false sense
of empowerment
and inclusion
by exercising
exclusion
i perceive
hegemonies
honed by hatred
where members only
are allowed
where all those unlike
are demonized
oppressed
and left behind
to restore
the reputation
of god

My Brand New Bible

my grandmother gave me her bible
in her will
and as i hold it now
i feel as if i'm breaking sacred trust
unsure if i'm even allowed to touch it
or if i'll ever dare to open it

for years it sat closed upon her coffee table
closed tight
its pristine white cover
emblazoned with gold leaf letters
to match its gilded pages

i'd stare at it for hours
imagining what magic lived inside
those pages edged with gold
i envisioned illuminated leaves
like a monk's medieval manuscript
and wondered how much holier their truths must be
how much more sublime their mysteries
than the humbler ones we had at home

but i never dared to touch it
out of fear my grandmother
in her stern godliness
would exercise her wrath
and punish me for staining or rustling the pages
with my *nasty little fingers*

holding it at last after all these years
i feel my grandmother's presence looming

above me rigid staunch stationary cold
and as the old fear and dread begin
to build in my lower back

i wonder if she'd ever opened it at all

THE POWER OF PRAYER

what would i have to say
    to a god
  worthy of the saying

and what could i do
    to be found
  worthy of the doing

so i sit at my keyboard
    trying
  trying

A Poem for William Blake

were the bible to be blessed with the book of william blake
it would change the course of christendom for the better
long after all the other prophets had faded into distant myth
long after all their calls for the coming of the christ had been
institutionalized clichéd and reified to the dumping ground of history
apocalyptic vision rose again in a man whose four-fold imagination
moved the conversation to england's green and present land

blake was first introduced to me through the words of lecturers
languishing in the error and blindness that is the theme of
all his work but i've since found the maker of the lamb and tyger is
kept from our restrained eyes so that we can finally see at albion's
emanation that all deities do indeed reside within the human breast

THESE THINGS AREN'T EASY

i am not a poet
of darkness depression
or despair
nor am i
a poet of light
i find beauty
in the dialectic
the struggle
between god and the world
and i have found
more beauty and dignity
more poetry
in harrison's v's
hemingway's nadas
and hardy's altar crumbs
than in herbert's easter wings
these things aren't easy
nor would i have it any other way

THE ROAD TO DEMOPOLIS

for louie skipper

i was on the road to demopolis
to meet an old friend
at a barbecue joint
when a light flashed from above
and a voice called my name
above the din of daydream
and dave matthews

i know why you persecute me

after making sure i was still
awake and on the road
i sheepishly asked

lord is that you

a voice more like jackie mason
than james replied

no i am paul the apostle
from the epistles
the one you've been persecuting
in your poems but let us fix
your eyes on me the real me
who is patient and kind
not the proud boastful
self-serving voice
you've always heard
i have faith that you can clear my name
and make me fully known

i asked why would i do that
and how when he cut in

i thought you could write
one of those jesus *poems of yours*
they're really about me anyway
i want you to stand your ground
against the powers of this dark world
bring condemnation to corruption
and open people's eyes

i tried to ask what one poem
could do but he interrupted

i've been accused of turning
the religion of *jesus into*
a religion about *jesus*
all because the ancient church
made a book and called it sacred
and built a new religion out of what
they took to be my religion

but i wasn't writing the bible
i was writing letters
answering questions
putting out fires in living
correspondence with friends

i objected that those letters
have been a major tool
in fueling fundamentalism
and the religious right
of undermining
the kingdom of christ
but he kept going

i was a product of my time
writing for my time
i was a revolutionary

but my words have been co-opted
revised and reduced to means
for irreligious ends

hell if i'd known i was writing
scripture *i wouldn't have*
mentioned some personal things
i was wrestling with
like that whole thing
about the thorn in my flesh

what an abomination that was

and many of the conservative parts
were added long after i was dead
just to push the conservative cause

you won't believe this but i agree
with what william blake and others
have said about me the evils
of a negative morality
of thou shalt nots
of a repressive morality
suppressing desire and imagination

life is nothing but desire
and imagination

what we need is
an expressive morality
that leads us into a life of doing
of desiring of imagining
the world as it should be
as god would have it to be
and making it so

THE HOLINESS TEMPLE OF IMMACULATE REDEMPTION

my church would have no preaching
no liturgy no praise
only lectionary and silence

bearing truths readings taken
from old testament lawgivers
like wordsworth and coleridge

shelley and keats from prophets
blake and rousseau emerson thoreau
new testament verses would draw

from dickinson rilke and clifton
stevens sanchez and dunn
while the gospel would be whitman

for never has word
been more truly of the lord
like tender oak leaves in spring

translucent luminescence
emerging from behind the viney veil
of dead and withered kudzu

Funeral in Early Spring

as the grave preacher recounts clichés
on the glories of eternal life a little girl
wanders off during her grandmother's funeral
a girl of three or four
in her brand-new easter bonnet bought
three days earlier with easter still weeks away

her mother had seemed hesitant
at the girl's insistence in wearing
pink and yellow lace and flowers
for such a solemn occasion

but harried after weeks in the hospital
watching her own mother fade
she gave in to her daughter's pleas
to wear the dress before its time

now beneath the preacher's words
the whispers grow among the spinsters
as they scowl at the audacity
of this splash of pink gliding
over the land of the dead

but the girl continues her dance
over the nearby graves
far too young to pretend to understand
what it means to die

she dances along
her dress catching the breeze
floating upward as if buoyed by the souls
the memories

the empty silences
of the dead
flowing softly
into the promise of her indifferent womb

Sermon on the Mount circa 2008

"This is a tremendous social crisis, greater even than the issue of slavery"
> —The Rev. Hayes Wicker on a proposed Florida
> state constitutional ban on same sex marriage
> *Naples Daily News*, April 17, 2008

i dreamt i watched
the sermon on the mount
live on fox news
of course jesus didn't look
anything like the haloed
angelic aryan passed down
through the centuries

his unkempt ragged beard
was punctuated with flowing dreadlocks
his skin was surprisingly dark
and his nose was distinctively jewish

his text was fairly faithful
straight out of matthew
slightly modernized from the rsv
however his preaching style
was unexpected he was not
the calm font of gentleness
from the movies
or stained-glass windows

he was shouting angry animated
perhaps even agitated
his tone was somewhere between
an inspired martin luther king
and an irate louis farrakhan

the crowd didn't like it at all
they seemed put off by his message
they even jeered and booed in places

the television graphics screamed
black preacher delivers radical address
and *jesus calls for redistribution of wealth*
then as he spoke of the meek's inheritance
the news crawl at the bottom cried out
palin attacks big government social programs

he ranted about turning
the other cheek as the chyron crawl
prophetically proclaimed
cheney calls for stronger stance on iraq

when jesus was getting to the part
about serving two masters
and judging others fox cut back
to bill o'reilly in the studio
who looked into the camera smirked
and with an *oh my god* expression
asked *can you believe this guy*

he complained how *this kind*
of radical garbage is just the start
of what we can expect under
an obama administration
the only way we can take
this country back is to return
to traditional american values

he then added *be sure to tune in tonight*
for my interview with reverend hayes wicker
who has made the most important statements to date
on the biggest issue currently facing our society

Rapture

i believe the rapture happened
the day my grandma died
no one else was good enough to go then
priests and preachers
the president and every one of us
were blatantly left behind
there were no reports
of vacated automobiles
or suddenly empty spots in line
the day of the rapture
was an uneventful day

on the day the rapture happened
god glanced at my grandmother
then looked down on his creation
at the squalor and ceaseless sin
the greed bitterness and war
the terror inflicted on all fronts
so often in his name under a blind
conviction that his will be done
he watched distracted
by the din of self-directed prayer
he turned toward her
with a sad repentant look
a tear ran down his radiant cheek
as he asked *what on earth have i done*

THE WAR ON CHRISTIANITY

they have been complaining for years
about the war on christianity
they are in the right

on the russian front the godless
communists attack with their
materialist academic dogma

terrors storm across the deserts
of northern africa and beyond
in clashes of imperialist rage

while even now truth justice
and american ideals
bombard the beaches of normandy

our hopes resting in the balance

PART OF GOD'S INCONCEIVABLE PLAN

*"A 20-year-old Pittsfield driver was cited by police
Tuesday after she ran down Lord Jesus Christ in a
marked crosswalk."*
         —*The Republican*, May 6, 2010

when the lord jesus christ
was struck by a car
in massachusetts did
the god half or man half prevail

did he stand against attack
stopping the car cold
saving vehicle and self
from injury and shame

or did he crumple under
machinery's progression
letting fly a few fucks as his body
became sacrifice to modernity

When We Made God

when we made god
    vanish
   in a puff of logic
we blamed it all on nietzsche,
or darwin
    i can't remember
but
we didn't need god
    we had technology for that
so
we started fighting wars over real
    important stuff
  assassinations
    living space
  free trade
  that's the biggie
    we had to make the world
safe for democracy
so
we imposed it
    on those who needed it
and
  of course
    like always
 we did it in the name of god
he's always there when we need him

A Word in the Beginning

a word in the beginning is the genesis of poetry
the finding of a single word can lead to musings

that grow into emotions and evolve into
what was once described as a spontaneous

overflow but there is no tranquility now
this is no time for poets to be mired

in transcendentia or romantic longings for
the reconciliation of our selves and our world

this had long been the realm of religion
but now we are left with politicians

who offer hope with nihilistic invocations
of jesus' name as just another empty word

but a word in the beginning can be a password
into primeval machinations of language itself

yet its genesis must be free of unnecessary
pedantry and eschew the sesquipedalian

it must transcend the mundanity of the diurnal
and whether it is like the song of the nightingale

or the blackbird whether it invokes the angels
of bethlehem or benjamin in the end

it must survive in the ritual of its recitation
in its becoming its reading its writing

THREE

And the Word Was God

TWILIGHT

twilight is a time
of intermingling light
and dark where beauty
resides however unwelcome
the victor predestined by the diurnal

an internecine drama
beyond the reach
of shakespeare's pen
or fellini's lens

a time that opens perception
inviting us to see
not in spite of the darkness
but because of it

a mockingbird behind me
impersonates the nightingale
and then the blackbird

i look for god
in the pages of a book
and find comfort
in the longing of duino
and dover beach

POEMS HAPPEN IN THE DARK

poems happen in the dark
when the pupils of perception
dilate to enlightenment
and allow what little light
there is to penetrate the darkness

poems happen in the dark
when dim and scattered beams of light
enlighten scattered places
and fight against the nothingness

poems happen in the dark
to show the way amid the shadows
to create stark contrasts
with the night
to save us from the days

THE LIFE OF THINGS

we don't need
trees and snow
angels
or even lakes or mountains
to see into the life of things
i've stood on the edge
of the grand canyon
in spring
breathless speechless
ridden through the alps
in summer
with yellow blooms
and waterfalls
driven through the rockies
in winter
mesmerized by snow
against a clear sunny sky
and i've seen
my four-year-old son
swinging
in the back yard
reaching to go high
enough to see over the bar
then returning
head tilted back
full of delight
laughing

Smoky Mountain Stream

facing upstream on a stone
in the middle of a smoky mountain
stream that splashes over its edges

gurgles between the rocks
gathers into pools
and murmurs its lazy way

through woods and hills
i enjoy the peaceful sounds
of water changing colors

from clear shimmering above
a creek bed of browns and greys
to the silver white of mini waterfalls

and back to clear again
for a moment i am wordsworth
communing with nature

just out of her reach
close enough to perceive
her wonders but far enough away

to stay safely out of touch
a collection of butterflies
congregates on a nearby stone

and the loveliest thing i see
all afternoon amid all of this
natural grandeur is the look

on my daughter's face
as she watches the butterflies
and just out of earshot mouths

they're so beautiful

CATHEDRAL

i've only been to the lake
three or four times since
my brother drew died
but i have often wondered
if he is still there
skiing through the narrows
like he always did
a single step off
the wooden platform
at the back of
the ski nautique
barefoot
with one leg crossed
over the other
as though he were sitting
in his own church pew
in his own cathedral
holding the rope handle
in the crook of his elbow
cigarette in one hand
and a miller high life in the other

if you're not out there
on the water now brother
i hope heaven is as good
as the lake would have been

When I Sing

when i sing i often feel
like a rich old woman
with a priceless steinway
in her front parlor
that she'd never learned how to play

i possess an instrument on which
i can bang out brilliant flourishes
fleeting fragments of virtuosity
that can at times approach
the heights of placido or pavarotti
or more often those of tonic or toad
like the young guitarist
who can dazzle
with a few zeppelin riffs
but cannot play an entire song

and as i sit here in virtual quietness
serenaded by the arrhythmic
almost inaudible clicks of this keyboard
i have a similar feeling as a poet

i have stashed away
somewhere in the attic
in one of the countless
boxes of books notebooks
and other sorts of literary trinkets
an antique ticket
for the train to transcendence
but i could never use it
the bridge is out near simplon pass
broken long ago

whether by the winds of time
or nietzsche's madman
i cannot be certain
but it is more likely that its abutments
and cross supports collapsed
under the weight of their own suppositions
or were gradually deconstructed
by internal contradictions
and faulty assumptions

and so we are left with the fragments
we can mimic the masterpieces
i have myself sung handel's messiah
haydn's creation and bach's b minor mass
and while
iambics often trickle off my tongue
i can only bang out fragments
on this keyboard

there is of course brief comfort
in attempts to imagine a stairway to heaven
but it is no different than the haunting rhythms
of the ocean or even the steps
of a fool in the rain

Beyond the Margins

even before
i'd read my milton
i'd tried to justify
the ways of god to men

i loved to float just
off the end of the pier
daydreaming
at eight or eighteen
endeavoring to understand

how god's will could be said
to allow a friend's mother
to have good light luck
on the way late to swim practice
while poverty hunger
and injustice lined
the streets she drove

how we could have freewill
when an omniscient god
foresaw everything
we would do even
before we were born

i'd grown up
in a christian environment
safe sheltered
nothing jesus freaky
just good solid methodism
i was encouraged
to speculate but not too far

i tested the bounds
of my allowable truths
but never dared to adventure
into darknesses beyond
the acceptable margins
never dared to consider
that i might have it all
backward

when that last set of doors
to the operating room closed
new doors opened

thoughts of how the tumor
in my brother's brain
could be the will of a god
worthy of my praise
overwhelmed the whiteness
of my innocence
with a spectral grey
ambivalent ubiquitous profound

AZALEA SPRING

azaleas paint the port
city in a signature sea
of pink perfection
the pride of mobile
splattered against growing
greens of early spring

while the haggard reverence
of mossy live oaks drape
this scene in subtle dignity
framing the timeless
character of the city

mobile's azalea trail curves
in endless arrhythmic lines
linking stately mansions
with humble cottages
throughout midtown

when easter comes early
the view from my porch
swing explodes
with significations
until these momentary
markers of dying march
wither to trodden
mottled nothingness
under the languid live oaks

ON LETTING GO THE TRANSCENDENTAL SIGNIFIED

i don't want to write
poems about jerking
off or fucking in a church

or in the ass i don't
want to write about
leaves or rocks pulled

out of boxes the feel
of felt or velvet or find
the perfect word

to personify the texture
of chocolate i'd prefer
to mine meanings of life

of love of truth but
the flaccid silhouette
of postmodernism

shrinks uselessly spent
in my rearview mirror
as shards of refracted

metaphysics dapple
its fading outlines
the way exclamations

fade to whispers after
satisfaction i want to
find large meanings

in even larger questions
but more important things
i find are left to write

SUNSET ON MOBILE BAY

as sunset swells behind
the mobile skyline
impossible oranges and reds
explode across the bay
amid silhouetted skyscrapers
shipyards and other shapes
reflecting on rippling waves

shakespeare and jesus
told how red and lowering
morning skies foretell
foul weather but here at sunset
they herald morning calm

from this deck of a restaurant
named for an interpretation
of the teachings of christ
that unite the virtues
of water sustenance truth

i find myself lost in musings
how infinite unrelenting
suggestions seem to stretch
straight up to our table
how beauty falls subject
to each of our perspectives
how meaning is unmoored
how such perceptions don't
have to mean anything at all

JUST OFF THE END OF THE PIER

for fay simpkins

wading swimming
treasure hunting
without goggles
we'd find pebbles sticks beer cans
and the occasional minnow or bream
in the green netherworld
beneath my friend david's pier

soon our searching grew
first by canoe
then our ropes were loosened
by a small flat-bottom fishing boat
that carried us through creeks
woods and ancient dwellings
at the ends of this or that slough

my friend david's mother
whom i also called mom
would sit with us on that pier
under the light of the stars
and the sometime moon
and thrill us with her musings
of ghosts and god and ufos

while two stargazing boys
sunburned on icarus wings
first explored the murky depths

OF SCHOOLS AND SCHOOLMASTERS

in response to re-reading chapter lxxxviii of
moby dick

drifting blindly in discursive
currents their bodies
buoyed by habit and hierarchy
below us mirror our forms

they roll about over the watery
world with insinuations
of submission roll through roles
of gender and subtle inseminations

of power and are put out to sea alone
the folly of so-called learning
the battle scars of so-called love
the emptiness of individuality

how long must we believe
biology shapes behavior
blaming our own oppressions
on whales

JIM'S PLACE

for jim gray

driving through a central florida swamp
listening to tony harrison read
of micanopy kumquats and john keats's joy's fruit

searching for deer we discover only cows
looking for herons find buzzards

what we do find however with the aid
of homemade mead and some red dog
stolen from some guy's porch fridge

is a place only a couple of miles from town
a few dozen yards off the highway a place

teeming with cowshit and mosquitoes a place
that allows two men distracted by the din
of daily living and modern politics to discover

aided by rilke's longing and harrison's *vs*
that savoring words is not dawdling but love

OBSEQUIES OF AUTUMN

in mid-november as
withered leaves relax

their hold on tired
indifferent branches and lethargic

clouds make their apathetic
western way a splash

of mockingbirds disturbs
the horizon a hawk waits

silent in the shadowed trees

Rhyming Landscapes

our world's a textual fabric written
and rewritten translated from perception

to consciousness for reading is reiteration
mere reification of artificial constructs

the world's a poem that doesn't rhyme
it lacks a certain metric or sense of time

the natural world wordsworth wrote of long ago
was harmony wrought in the style of church hymns

or flowing lines of tintern abbey and the ode
immortal harmony and beauty we no longer see

the world's a poem that doesn't rhyme
it lacks a certain metric or sense of time

wordsworth's accounts of early spring
and daffodils come from the perspective

of outside observer as though he wrote
while looking out a window or at a painting

the world's a poem that doesn't rhyme
it lacks a certain metric or sense of time

we can no longer write wordsworth's garden
for nature is nothing but the perpetual exercise

of sex and violence where wolves run through
evergreen forests and dormant kudzu drapes

the world like grey cobwebs in a haunted attic
like a poem that doesn't rhyme

DEEP THOUGHTS

recently someone determined once and for all
that tomatoes are in fact vegetables

which simply shows once and for all

that there is no place for once and for all
now you might smirk and say the state

of tomatoes is pretty trivial ground

for such weighty philosophical determinations
however such things are not unusual for someone

who had a revelation about the existence of god

in biology class where a discussion of fruit
brought all things suddenly out of focus

and since that day i've not been able to understand

how the blind forces of evolution
which i had long taken as a matter of faith

could have ever conceived of a commercialization

system for seeds how seeds could be situated
into a piece of fruit encased in a seductive orb

of vivacious color and sensuous sweetness

in order that an unwitting animal might
be lured to partake unaware of the tiny bits

of potential life hidden inside safely strategically

steeled against the destructive forces of digestion
how all of this could be part of a clandestine

conspiracy to bring forth new life by placing it

into a ready-made system for its germination
into a rich self-fertilizing bed of nourishment

and how the very crux of our metaphysical

and ideological foundations how the key to all
understanding could really just be a pile of crap

WHEN SKIES ARE GREY

we wish our lives awash in sunlight
believing the beautiful days
are clear skied and fair yet i
driving home in intermittent rain
behold this scene
the world around me
bathed in the spirit of warm
black storm clouds
luminously sublimely ominous

for this north alabama landscape
normally bland in late winter
is painted in a fluorescent beauty
colors more vivid
contrasts more defined
especially the greens
the incremental nascent greens
of coming spring

i've noticed this too
in michigan in early may
with the tulips and maturing leaves
but here in late february
with the dull prosaic
greys and browns of
naked hardwoods
the greys and yellows of
hay and dormant kudzu
creating contrasts with the evergreens
and greening grass

and i remember rilke
how beauty is as close
to terror as we can possibly endure

you must feel to live

NOTES

p. 3   The Day I Was Born
This poem was originally published in *The Pea River Journal.*

p. 4   Lost Cause
This poem was originally published in *The Pea River Journal.*

p. 5-7   I Wish That I Were Langston Hughes
This poem was originally published in *I Wish That I Were Langston Hughes.*

Song of Myself, Walt Whitman, 1855.

"White Privilege: Unpacking the Invisible Knapsack," Peggy McIntosh, © 1988.

"Lines Composed a Few Miles Above Tintern Abbey, on Revisiting the Banks of the Wye During a Tour. July 13, 1798," William Wordsworth, 1798.

"I, Too," Langston Hughes, © 1925.

"Nikki-Rosa," Nikki Giovanni, © 1968.

"Yet Do I Marvel," Countee Cullen, © 1925.

"I Know Why the Caged Bird Sings," Maya Angelou, © 1969.

"Harlem," Langston Hughes, © 1951.

"Coal," Audre Lorde, © 1968.

"Can the Subaltern Speak?" Gayatri Spivak, © 1988.

"The Fact of Blackness," Frantz Fanon, © 1952.

"We Wear the Mask," Paul Laurence Dunbar, 1896.

Hamlet, William Shakespeare, 1601

The Wasteland, T. S. Eliot, © 1922.

p. 8-9   The Road to the Lake
This poem was originally published in *DREW: Poems from Blue Water.*

p. 10   Humidity
This poem was originally published in *The Pea River Journal.*

p. 11   To Sing of the South
This poem was originally published in *The Oracle.*

p. 14   Architectural Inequities
To Kill a Mockingbird, Harper Lee, © 1960.

p. 17   Love Poem #2
"White Privilege: Unpacking the Invisible Knapsack," Peggy McIntosh, © 1988.

p. 18   Scars of Segregation
Commonly attributed to William Butler Yeats, but source unknown.

p. 22-23 Our Country Is Broken
On Liberty, John Stuart Mill, 1843.

"The New Colossus," Emma Lazarus, 1883.

The Gay Science, Friedrich Nietzsche, 1882.

p. 27   Jesus Walks the Southland
This poem was originally published in *The 2008 Anthology for The Limestone Dust Poetry Festival* and *The Oracle.*

"Musée des Beaux Arts," W. H. Auden, © 1938.

p. 29-30 Building Kingdoms
The Marriage of Heaven and Hell, William Blake, 1793.

Luke 17:20.

p. 34   The Power of Prayer
         The SAGE Handbook of Qualitative Research, Norman Denzin
         and Yvonna Lincoln, © 2005.

p. 35   A Poem for William Blake
         This poem was originally published in *I Wish That I Were
         Langston Hughes*.

         Milton: A Poem, William Blake, 1810.

         The Marriage of Heaven and Hell, William Blake, 1793.

         Songs of Innocence and of Experience, William Blake, 1789.

         Jerusalem, William Blake, 1821.

p. 36   These Things Aren't Easy
         This poem was originally published in *DREW: Poems from
         Blue Water.*

         v., Tony Harrison, © 1982.

         "A Clean, Well-Lighted Place," Ernest Hemingway, © 1926.

         "Channel Firing," Thomas Hardy, © 1914.

         "Easter Wings," George Herbert, 1633.

p. 37-39 The Road to Demopolis
         *The First Paul: Reclaiming the Radical Visionary Behind the
         Church's Conservative Icon*, Marcus J Borg and John Dominic
         Crossan, © 2009.

         Acts 9:4.

         Hebrews 12:2.

p. 41-42 Funeral in Early Spring
         "Easter Parade," Irving Berlin, © 1933.

p. 48   When We Made God
The Hitchhiker's Guide to the Galaxy, Douglas Adams, © 1979.

The Gay Science, Friedrich Nietzsche, 1882.

On the Origin of Species, Charles Darwin, 1859.

Mein Kampf, Adolph Hitler, © 1925.

Address to Congress, Woodrow Wilson, © 1917.

p. 49   A Word in the Beginning

"Preface to Lyrical Ballads," William Wordsworth, 1800.

Song of Myself, Walt Whitman, 1855.

"Ode to a Nightingale," John Keats, 1819.

"Thirteen Ways of Looking at a Blackbird," Wallace Stevens, © 1917.

Theses on the Philosophy of History, VII, Walter Benjamin, © 1950.

p. 53   Twilight
This poem was originally published in *DREW: Poems from Blue Water.*

"Ode to a Nightingale," John Keats, 1819.

"Thirteen Ways of Looking at a Blackbird," Wallace Stevens, ©1917.

The Duino Elegies, Rainer Maria Rilke, © 1922.

"Dover Beach," Matthew Arnold, 1867.

p. 54   Poems Happen in the Dark
This poem was originally published in *DREW: Poems from Blue Water.*

p. 55   The Life of Things
         "Birches," Robert Frost, © 1915.

         "Stopping by Woods on a Snowy Evening," Robert Frost, © 1923.

         The Duino Elegies, Rainer Maria Rilke, © 1922.

         "Lines Composed a Few Miles Above Tintern Abbey, on Revisiting
         the Banks of the Wye During a Tour. July 13, 1798," William
         Wordsworth, 1798.

p. 58   Cathedral
         Versions of this poem were originally published in *DREW: Poems
         from Blue Water* and *The Birmingham Arts Journal.*

p. 59-60 When I Sing
         This poem was originally published in I *Wish That I Were
         Langston Hughes.*

         The Prelude William Wordsworth, 1850.

         The Gay Science, Friedrich Nietzsche, 1882.

         "Structure, Sign, and Play in the Discourse of the Human
         Sciences," Jacques Derrida, © 1966.

         The Messiah, George Friedrich Handel, 1742.

         The Creation, Joseph Haydn, 1798.

         Mass in B Minor, Johann Sebastian Bach, 1749.

         "Stairway to Heaven," Jimmy Page and Robert Plant, © 1971.

         "The Ocean," John Bonham, John Paul Jones, Jimmy Page, and
         Robert Plant, © 1973.

         "Fool in the Rain," John Paul Jones, Jimmy Page, and Robert
         Plant, © 1979.

p. 61-62   Beyond the Margins
This poem was originally published in *DREW: Poems from Blue Water.*

Paradise Lost, John Milton, 1667.

p. 63   Azalea Spring
A version of this poem was originally published in *Literary Mobile,* 10th Anniversary Edition, © 2013.

p. 64   On Letting Go the Transcendental Signified
A version of this poem was originally published in *F*CK Poems: An Exceptional Anthology,* © 2012.

Of Grammatology, Jacques Derrida, translated by Gayatri Chakravorty Spivak, © 1974.

p. 65   Sunset on Mobile Bay
The Compleat Angler, or the Contemplative Man's Recreation, Izaak Walton, 1653.

p. 66   Just Off the End of the Pier
A version of this poem was originally published in *DREW: Poems from Blue Water.*

p. 67   Of Schools and Schoolmasters
This poem was originally published as a part of the *Remaking Moby-Dick Project,* © 2013.

p. 68   Jim's Place

"A Kumquat for John Keats," Tony Harrison, © 1979.

"Ode on Melancholy," John Keats, 1819.

The Duino Elegies, Rainer Maria Rilke, © 1922.

p. 70   Rhyming Landscapes
"Lines Composed a Few Miles Above Tintern Abbey, on Revisiting the Banks of the Wye During a Tour. July 13, 1798," William Wordsworth, 1798.

"Ode: Intimations of Immortality from Recollections of Early Childhood," William Wordsworth, 1804.

p. 73   When Skies Are Grey
A version of this poem was originally published in *DREW: Poems from Blue Water,* © 2009.

The Duino Elegies, Rainer Maria Rilke, © 1922.

Made in the USA
Charleston, SC
13 May 2014